THE Life OF AN Olive

D. Yael Bernhard

HelioTween

New York City

*"There is no more passionate tree anywhere,
nothing that relates to man, like an olive."*

– Mort Rosenblum,
Olives: The Life & Lore of a Noble Fruit

The author gratefully acknowledges the following individuals who helped create this book: Dani Livney of Kibbutz Gezer, Israel; Raquelle Noymeir of Rish Lakish olive press, Tzipori, Israel; Yigal Sela, olive historian; Jan Bang; Patches Livney; Varda Livney; Melissa Milgram, Ronnie Herman; Jonathan Follender; Rabbi Jonathan Kligler; David Charles Ross; Gwen Tapper; Julie Makowsky; Miriam Safira-Simon; Allison Ofanasky; Karen Levine; Chana Lunior; Tikva Fischzang; and Professor Shimon Lavee of the Hebrew University of Jerusalem.

Designed and typeset by D. Yael Bernhard

For Dani Livney,
olive grower, picker, pruner,
pickler, and eater

The Olive Tree's Lifespan

Territories of the Twelve Tribes of Jacob

1200 BCE

Naphtali

Asher

Manasseh

Zebulun

Issachar

Kinneret (Sea of Galilee)

Manasseh

Jordan River

Gad

Ephraim

Benjamin

Dan

Jerusalem

Reuben

Judah

Dead Sea

Simeon

Negev Desert

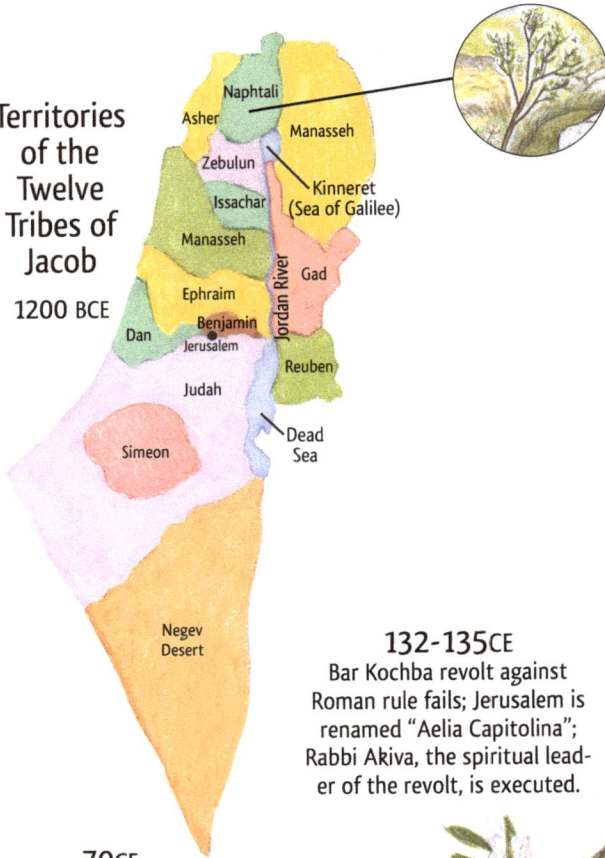

Ancient olive press using stone weights

333-633CE
Christian churches are built throughout the Holy Land following the ambitions of Queen Helena, mother of Constantine

634-638CE
Jerusalem is conqured by Muslim leader Caliph Omar; Palestine becomes Islamic territory

1187-1291CE
Saladin, first Mameluk Sultan of Egypt & Syria, defeats the Crusaders

132-135CE
Bar Kochba revolt against Roman rule fails; Jerusalem is renamed "Aelia Capitolina"; Rabbi Akiva, the spiritual leader of the revolt, is executed.

70CE
The Roman Empire conquers Jerusalem and renames Israel "Palestina". Second Temple falls; Jewish residents are sent into exile.

70-130CE
Rabbi Akiva & Rabbi ben Zakkai establish the first synagogues throughout the land.

325CE
Emperor Constantine of Byzanthium (known as Turkey today) converts to Christianity and recognizes Palestine as the Holy Land

100-200CE
The Gospels of Mark, Luke, Matthew and John are written, including the Sermon on the Mount.

570CE
Birth of the Prophet Muhammed, founder of Islam, in the Arabian city of Mecca (now in Saudi Arabia)

1099CE
Crusaders from Europe establish a kingdom in Jerusalem and reestablish Christian rule in The Holy Land

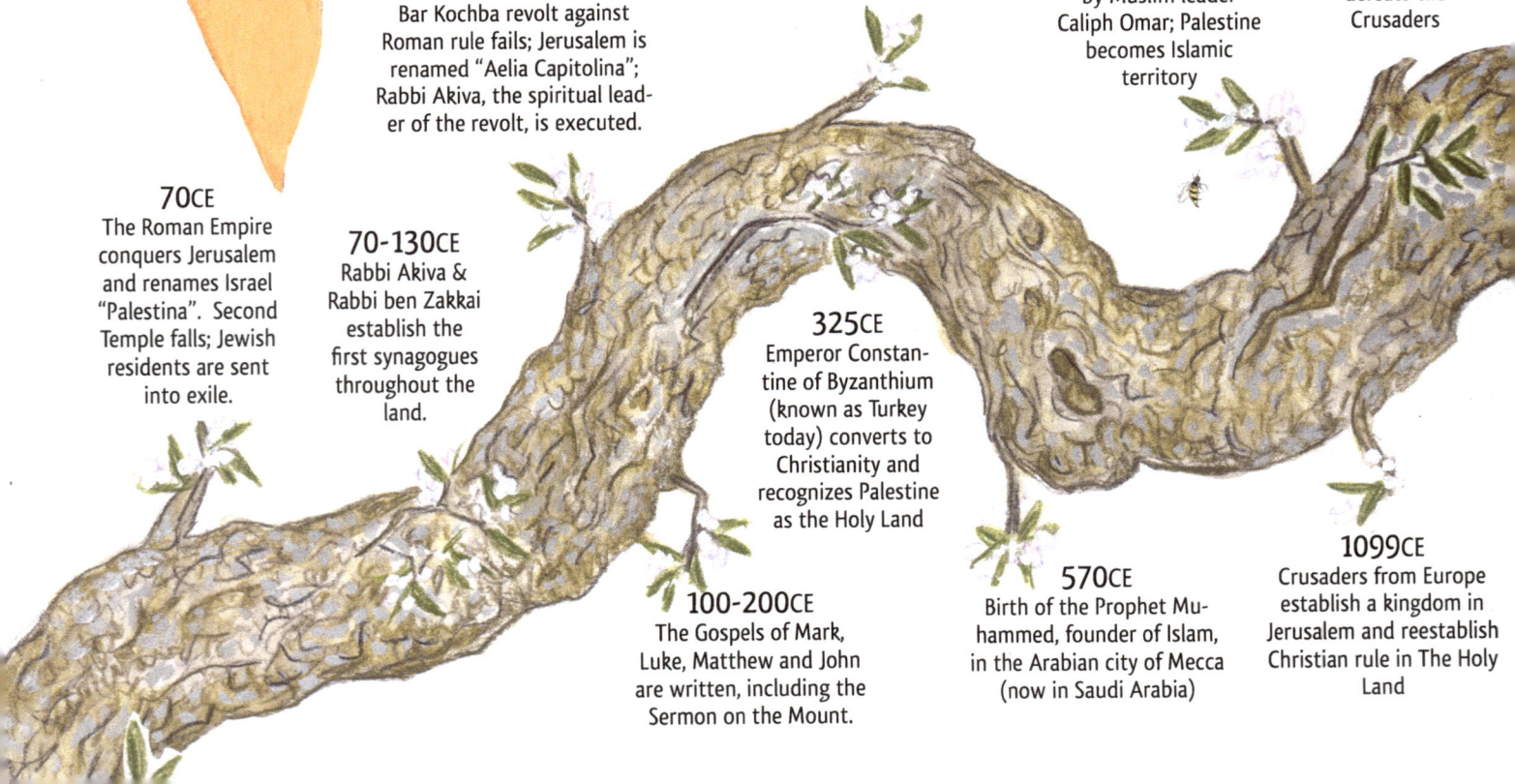

1917CE
WWI brings Ottoman rule to an end; the Balfour Declaration transfers authority over Palestine to Great Britain

1948-1960CE
Hundreds of thousands of Jews are expelled from North African, Arab & Persian lands, and seek refuge in Israel.

1904-1948CE
The Second Aliyah: Millions of European Jews seek refuge from WWII and the Holocaust in Europe

2016CE
Israel stands as the only democracy in the Middle East, with thriving agriculture and continuing trade in olives.

1948CE
Great Britain turns Palestine over to the United Nations, which votes to partition the land into the State of Israel and Trans-Jordan. Israel wins a two-year War of Independence against the local Arab population, who reject the Partition Plan.

1967CE
Israel is attacked by five Arab nations in the Six Day War; wins the war and gains the territories of Judea & Samaria (the West Bank), the Sinai Peninsula, and the Golan Heights.

1516CE
Palestine becomes part of the Ottoman Empire under Suleiman the Magnificent, who offers refuge to Jews fleeing Europe

1880-1900CE
The First Aliyah: Jewish immigrants arrive in Palestine from Yemen, Eastern Europe & Russia; the first railroad to Jerusalem is built, and construction of Tel Aviv begins.

1500-1600CE
Jewish mysticism (Kabbalah) begins to thrive in Tzfat (Safed), northern Israel among Sephardic Jews

1492CE
Over 350,000 Sephardic Jews are expelled from Spain by King Ferdinand & Queen Isabella; many flee to Palestine

500-year-old olive press using stone wheel pulled by donkey

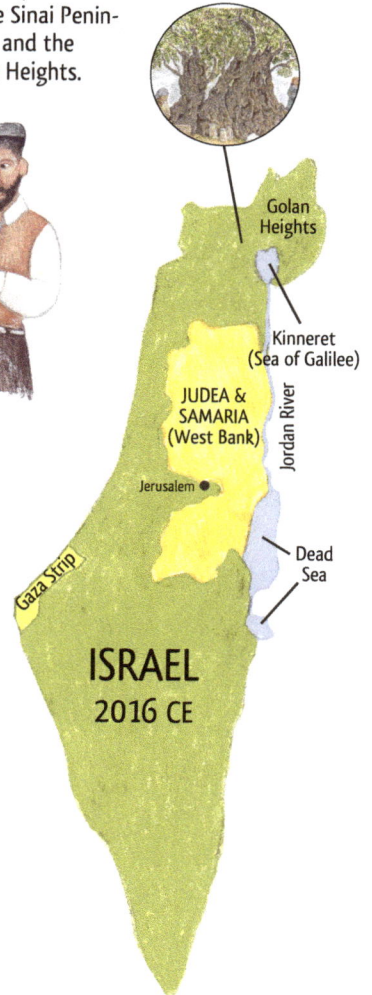

Golan Heights

Kinneret (Sea of Galilee)

JUDEA & SAMARIA (West Bank)

Jordan River

Jerusalem

Dead Sea

Gaza Strip

ISRAEL
2016 CE

Plip, plop. On a grassy slope in the Galilee, in the 70th year of the Common Era, an olive falls from a tree. It bounces off the cheek of a man sleeping on the ground, then rolls to the earth.

Ya'akov opens one eye and sees the ripe olive laying next to him. Ya'akov is hungry, but he knows he cannot eat this small fruit called *zayit* straight from the tree, for it is too bitter, and must be pickled first.

Ya'akov has traveled on foot for four cycles of the moon, far from the flames of Jerusalem where the Romans tore down the Temple – far from a home Ya'akov knows he will not see again.

As Ya'akov stretches and stands, his foot presses the fallen olive into a crack in the earth. New, green grass, enlivened by the first rain of the season, pokes up through brown grass. Under the dry grass the air is hot.

After two days the olive begins to dry and pucker. Ya'akov is rested and his water pouch is full, but as he looks out over the valley, he decides to stay. Week after week, the olive lies under the grass, its skin purple-grey and wrinkled. Week after week, Ya'akov gathers stones to build a sheepfold, his skin brown from working in the sun.

Months pass, then a year. New rains fall. The olive pit begins to soften and swell.

Soon a tender shoot sprouts from the olive pit. It pushes up through the soil and unfolds its first leaves toward the sun.

*S*woosh! The little olive tree trembles and sways as it is swatted by a woolly tail. A few tiny white flowers flutter to the ground. It is the tree's fifth spring-time – the 77th year of the Common Era.

The slender olive is nearly stepped on by the sheep that stop to graze, but the big rock beside it protects it. The young sapling bends in the breeze that blows through the valley, carrying with it the sound of a shepherd's lyre. Ya'akov's daughter Gilah plucks the strings and hums a tune as the animals graze on wild amaranth. A bee hovers among the olive blossoms, then flies away.

The little olive tree grows in the hot sun. It is rooted in a land long known as the territory of the tribe of Naphtali, the sixth son of Jacob, in the Kingdom of Israel. Its new name, *Palaestina* – Land of the Sea People – was given by the Greeks who conquered it four centuries ago, and by the Romans who now rule these fruitful valleys.

Nearly seven years since the burning of Jerusalem, Gilah sings of the beautiful Temple that was destroyed. In its place, smaller synagogues are springing up throughout the land, along with Roman temples, and statues of the emperor from across the sea.

On a sunny autumn day in the year 100 CE, Shimon reaches up through the dry leaves and plucks a pale olive. He holds the hard fruit between two fingers, rubbing its chalky skin until it shines. The olive tree is twenty eight years old. Shimon's grandfather, Ya'akov, gestures toward the ripening olives as he and his friends discuss the proper way to harvest. "Picking olives by beating the tree with a stick may save time," he says, "but it breaks branches. One should not beat a tree like it's a stubborn camel."

"Perhaps," another man answers, "if the olive tree must give something up, then so should the picker. Any fruit on a branch that breaks and falls should be given to the poor."

"King Solomon himself used 'beaten oil' to pay for the cedars of Lebanon that were used to build the Temple", argues a third. "Are we to rule against what our wise king allowed?"

"King Solomon gave generously to the poor," answers Ya'akov.

Shimon listens as day after day, the elders debate the meaning of the Torah and its commandments. How should they interpret the ancient words that will guide their people into the future?

Shimon sees a flock of white doves rise from a tree and turn as one into the sunshine. It is hard to believe that beyond this peaceful valley, there is so much unrest in the land. Cities have been captured, buildings and streets burned and rebuilt with Roman names. Thousands have fled to other lands. More than ever, the teachings must be gathered and preserved, just like the fruit of this tree that Shimon will soon help harvest.

The year is 132 CE. Cries in the night mingle with the clash of metal and the smell of smoke. Roman soldiers spread out through the valley, setting fire to peoples' homes. Ya'akov's great great granddaughter Tziporah flees with her mother in the dark. They pass the olive tree as the grassy slope catches fire. The tree is engulfed in flames. Tziporah covers her head as burning branches fall to the ground.

When the people are gone and the flames turn to smoke and ash, the olive tree appears dead. Its trunk is badly charred, and the upper roots are singed. But under the hard earth, the deeper roots are still alive.

Tziporah and her family flee to the north. Like the olive tree, their home is burned, but their roots will survive. With time, they will return.

The olive tree does not bear fruit this season. It waits quietly for human hands to cut away the dead wood. Only then can the tree begin to grow and thrive again.

The year is 172. Now a century old, the olive tree is forgotten. A trader stops to rest after a brief snowstorm. His donkey is laden with heavy sacks of colored stones, to be crushed for paint or cut into tiles for mosaics. The trader does not linger, wishing to reach the nearby city of Tzfat before the Sabbath.

A gerbil darts quickly into a crack in the olive tree as a shaggy brown bear pushes its strong nose under rocks and into holes, looking for insects and honeybees. A short-toed eagle watches from a tall cedar, then lifts its wings and takes off, soaring over the valley.

As time passes, the olive tree's bark folds itself into unique curves, holes, and bulges. Its strong roots soak up winter rains and melting snow. At the base of the blackened trunk, slender new trunks begin to sprout, but they do not bear fruit. The new growth is home to ladybugs, ants, and a tiny chameleon.

As dusk falls, a mongoose waddles by, searching for a fat mouse or a juicy lizard to eat – or even a slithery snake.

The summer of 370 is hot. James takes a pruning hook from his belt, and cuts the tender green shoots that sprout from the fork of a large limb of the olive tree, competing for sunlight.

James notices movement on the hillside. A shy gazelle is grazing among the rocks. Far in the distance, pilgrims move along the road. Earlier today, James saw a pair of donkeys dragging a large log, freshly cut and bound for the ceiling of the new church in Nazareth. James remembers his grandfather's stories about his ancestors

who came to
this valley from
Jerusalem cen-
turies ago, during
the Great Revolt. He
wonders if they picked
olives from this very
tree.

A scarlet dragonfly hovers
near James as he prunes the
shoots at the base of the thick trunk. He
keeps several cuttings to transplant. They will grow
into new olive trees.

Now James chops away the old, dead wood with his
axe. He spreads sheep manure around the base of the
trunk. He smiles and wipes his forehead. James
knows the olive tree will be healthier now,
and its new growth will yield
more fruit.

Tomorrow is the Sabbath,
and both farmer and tree
will rest.

In the autumn of 632, Yemima slips her fingers into the hard tips of four goat horns, then reaches up and uses them to rake the olives from the slender branches. Green and purple olives thump to the ground. Two children whack the branches with sticks, racing each other to knock down the most fruit. The women chat in the shade as they sort olives, trading news of their families and recipes for curing sickness. The men discuss the rains to come and the faraway siege of Jerusalem. Everyone has seen riders on horses along the road to the coastal city of Akko, men who bring a new language and a new religion from the Arabian peninsula.

The olive tree is now over five hundred years old, yet the sound of its falling fruit is as plentiful as drops of rain, mingling with the soft breeze in the old tree's leaves. Now Yemima lifts the corners of the ground cloth and helps load the olives onto a cart. These will be crushed into an oily paste under a huge granite wheel, then pressed between woven mats under heavy weights until the precious oil runs out. The olive oil that anoints emperors and kings will also sustain Yemima's family and light their lamps through the coming winter. She does not know who will rule this land next, but she does know that if the olive trees are blessed, then so too are the people who depend on them.

The year is 1106. Miryam watches as her mother shows her how to crack olives between two stones. Then she drops them into a jar of water. The family needs to buy salt for pickling the olives, but it is too dangerous to travel to market. Bedouins on the road from Akko tell of a great fortress being built. Crusaders in armor and pilgrims in great numbers have journeyed from Europe to conquer the Holy Land. But to Miryam, this land is simply known as *Eretz Yisrael*: The Land of Israel.

The olive tree has stood in this valley for over a thousand years. Its trunk thickens as it grows. Dark cracks fold inward like a face; roots curl like fingers and toes. Between those gnarly feet, Miryam notices a shiny object wedged into the ground. She pokes the object and it comes loose. It is a small piece of pale quartz. Miryam studies the crystal, wiping it clean with the hem of her tunic. Then, reaching into the trunk, she presses it into a deep crevice. Even if the crusaders take her family's home, Miryam knows her secret treasure will be safe inside the olive tree.

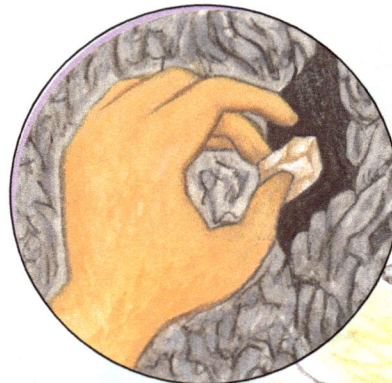

In the winter of 1291, Yaqub leans against the olive trunk, carving a piece of wood. A winter storm is coming; Yaqub can feel it. The soft branches above him wave in the wind like hair. To Yaqub, the whole tree is a living sculpture.

Yaqub sees a hoopoe bird hopping along the ground, pecking at fallen olives with its long beak. Toward the coast, dark clouds are gathering – or is it smoke? Fighting has broken out in the port city of Akko. Mamelukes from Egypt want to take back the Holy Land. But nestled deep in this valley, Yaqub's home feels safe.

Yaqub holds up his carving. The wide, flat spoon will be used for skimming olive oil from the tops of big jugs. For many generations, Yaqub's grandmother told him, their family has passed down their recipes for pickling and pressing olives.

Now Yaqub carves his name into the bark of the tree. Someday, he hopes, his own children and grandchildren will add their names to this ancient olive tree.

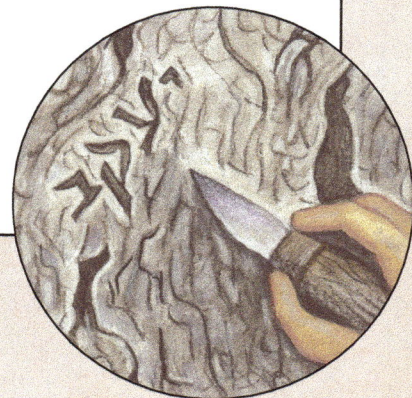

The year is 1570. Ester dips her hands into a bowl of ground fiber left over from pressing olives. She shapes the crumbly mash between her hands, pressing it into flat cakes. Then she lays the cakes in the sun to dry. Her brother Ezra sits beside her, studying a scroll.

Ester looks up through the branches of the unfamiliar tree. Her family traveled here all the way from Spain, leaving their home to find a safer place to live. Here on the far shores of the sea, they have found refuge in this valley named Ein Zeitim: Source of Olives.

The family sings songs of gratitude and hope – and for once, they do not have to sing in secret. Ezra will be able to study with the Kabbalists in nearby Tzfat. Just as they did at home, Ester's family will harvest olives, pickle them for eating, and press them for oil. They will burn the oil for light and the cakes of mash for cooking fuel. They will make medicines from the leaves, charcoal from pruned branches, and carve cups and spoons from the wood. Like the trees they left behind, this ancient one will help sustain the family. In return, they will honor and care for the olive tree.

Ester peers into the sunken holes of the hollow trunk. A faint twinkle catches her eye. She reaches in and dislodges a small crystal embedded in the bark. She rubs it with olive oil until the pale brown quartz shines. Ester puts the crystal in her hidden pocket, where a special pebble has traveled with her for many months. Now she has a new treasure in her new home!

It is autumn in the year 1892. Ida and Yankel bring water to fill the glass jars sitting in the shade of the olive tree. Singing in Yiddish, the twins' mother picks an olive from a basket, cuts an "x" in the fruit with a small knife, and drops it in a jar. These olives will soak in salt water to pickle them for eating. Other olives are stuffed into burlap bags and taken to the press, where two oxen push the heavy wooden shaft that turns the wheel that crushes the olives. Yankel loves to watch the thin stream of oil running into a basin beneath the great stones.

The children have seen many new things on their long journey from Belarus. Riding on the brand new train from Jaffa to Jerusalem, they met many people traveling to Palestine: a professor from the Ukraine, a doctor from Lithuania, a merchant from Bulgaria; and from the south, Yemenite Jews who want to build a whole new city on the coast called Tel Aviv. Like multicolored olives, people from many nations gather in this land where the ancient olive tree has now lived for eighteen centuries. Ida and Yankel miss their homeland, but they look forward to their new lives in *Eretz Yisrael*.

On a spring day in 1948, David settles into the gentle curve of an olive branch. Tiny green olives hide among the leaves, casting spotted shadows. Through the gnarly branches, David spots a jeep driving along the grassy slope, avoiding the road where a line of British vehicles retreats toward the coast. The jeep stops. The driver raises binoculars to watch the trucks go. David watches too, and smiles. Yesterday this tree stood in a country called Palestine; now for the second time in its long life, it is part of Israel again. Yet the region is also home to new arrivals from neighboring countries, as well as Europe, southern Asia, north Africa and even America. Many people seek refuge from war; others wish to join the *kibbutzim* that thrive throughout the Galilee. New homes appear in the valley. Mixed languages are spoken along the road . . . but David recognizes the man in the jeep as a Palmach soldier. Like his

uncle Jack, David hopes to join the Palmach someday, too.

David spies a lizard perched on a mossy patch of bark, and tries to grab it. The tree is also home to a soft juniper skink, a brown hare, and a colorful bee eater. Sometimes David hears the lone call of a fox. He knows his ancestors lived in this valley long, long ago. David wonders: did they catch lizards too?

On a grassy slope in the Galilee in the year 2016 CE, an olive tree lives. Almost two thousand years have passed since the tree first sprouted from a pit. Yet the tree still produces abundant fruit, and its young leaves flutter against the ancient bark.

Leaning against the massive trunk, Yakov picks up a guitar and strums a tune from ancient times. Friends and neighbors sit around a large tarp full of olives harvested from the tree. From a valley to the southeast, a Palestinian olive grower arrives to join the harvest crew. Yakov met him at the olive

press. The two growers shake hands. They share stories of the harvest as the workers sort through the olives, picking out broken twigs, stray leaves, and an occasional grasshopper. Then the olives are poured into crates, loaded onto a trailer, and hitched to a tractor.

Two pickers arrive on foot with backpacks full of bread and cheese, cucumbers and tomatoes, yogurt, and freshly-pressed olive oil. Yakov leans his guitar against the tree and joins the picnic. The harvest is good. The oil is rich and hearty. The pickers are hungry and happy.

As the harvest crew walks home, the sun sets and the air is sweet with the fragrance of olive leaves. A fruit bat darts past the ancient olive tree, black as the ink on a scroll against the sky.

Under the olive tree, a single olive drops to the earth and settles into the grass. From the far side of the valley, an owl calls.

Inside a nearby home, someone pauses to listen.

Glossary

aliyah	Hebrew for "going up"; a Jewish term for immigrating to Israel
ancestor	a relative from the distant past from whom a person or family has descended
anoint	to rub with oil as part of a religious ceremony
Arab	someone whose ancestors may be traced back to the Arabian Peninsula
Babylon	an ancient city of Mesopotamia on the banks of the Euphrates River
Bedouin	a nomadic Arab tribe of the desert
bee-eater	a brightly-colored bird that hunts flying insects, especially bees
century	a period of one hundred years
charcoal	a piece of solid black carbon left over when wood is burned, used as cooking fuel
commandment	a divine rule meant to be faithfully obeyed
Common Era	the period of time that began with what is believed to be the year Jesus Christ was born (also known as CE or AD: "After Death"; BCE indicates "Before Common Era")
crusade	a war mounted by the Catholic Church in the 11th, 12th, and 13th centuries to win the Holy Land back from Muslim rule
Eretz Yisrael	Hebrew for "The Land of Israel"
Galilee	a northern region of Israel west of the Jordan River, associated with Jesus Christ
granite	a very hard type of rock often used as a building material
Holy Land	a Christian name for the Land of Israel and east of the Jordan River, where Biblical events are believed to have taken place
Kabbalist	a person who studies or practices Jewish mysticism, or *Kabbalah*
kibbutz	a communal settlement in Israel, often a type of farm (plural: *kibbutzim*)
lyre	a stringed instrument like a harp, commonly used in ancient Greece and Mesopotamia
Mameluke	a group of slaves that rose to power in the 13th century and ruled in Syria, Israel, and Egypt

Mesopotamia	an ancient region between the Tigris and Euphrates Rivers, presently known as Iraq
mongoose	a small meat-eating animal with short legs and a long body and tail
mosaic	a picture or pattern created by arranging small pieces of colored stone, tile, or glass
Orthodox	strictly traditional or religious in lifestyle and practice
Palestine or Palaestina	the name given to Israel by Greek invaders in the 3rd century BCE and later by Roman rulers, referring to the Philistines who invaded the region in the 12th century BCE
Palestinian	any person who lived in Palestine from the time of Greek rule until the State of Israel was formed in 1948; today refers to Arabs who live in Judea and Samaria, also known as the West Bank and Gaza or "Palestinian territories"
Palmach	a secret fighting force formed in 1941 by Jewish communities in Palestine to resist British rule and help form the new State of Israel
peninsula	a piece of land surrounded on three sides by water
pilgrim	a person who journeys to a sacred place for religious reasons
siege	a military plan in which an army surrounds a city in order to cut off the people's supplies and force them to surrender
skink	a smooth-bodied lizard with short legs that burrows in sandy earth
Solomon	the son of King David, who became the second ruler of Israel in 1970 BCE. King Solomon was known as a wise ruler who built the First Temple in Jerusalem
synagogue	a building where Jews assemble for worship and learning (*beit knesset* in Hebrew)
Temple	either of two massive religious buildings of the Jews built on Mt. Moriah in Jerusalem. The First Temple was built by King Solomon in 957 BCE and destroyed by the Babylonian ruler Nebuchadnezzar in 586 BCE. The Second Temple was built in 515BCE, enlarged by Herod the Great in 20 BCE, and destroyed by the Romans in 70 CE. All that remains is the Western Wall, the holiest site for all Jews, also known as the Wailing Wall or *Kotel* in Hebrew.
Torah	the Hebrew Bible, also known as the Five Books of Moses, the Pentateuch (a Greek term), or the Old Testament (a Christian term). The Torah still exists as hand-written parchment scrolls in every synagogue, or may be read in a printed book called a *chumash*.
Yemenite	someone who lives in or whose ancestors come from the country of Yemen on the Arabian peninsula
Yiddish	a language invented by Eastern European Jews that blends German and Hebrew. Today it is mainly spoken by Orthodox Jews in Israel, Russia, and the U.S.

Facts About Olives

• An olive tree is a flowering evergreen tree which does not lose its leaves in winter. It is native to ancient Persia and Mesopotamia, and grows today all over the Middle East as well as the Arabian peninsula, southern Europe, north Africa, South Africa, southern Asia, Chile, Argentina, New Zealand, Australia, Java, India, Bermuda and California

• The most common species of olive is *olea europaea*, meaning "european olive", from the family of trees oleaceae.

• The word "oil" in many languages is derived from the word "olive".

• The seed inside an olive pit can take one to several years to germinate.

• An olive fruit is known as a *drupe*, a fleshy fruit with thin skin and a central stone containing the seed. Other examples of drupes are plums, cherries, and almonds.

• Olives turn from green to lavender to mauve to black as they ripen. Olives are very bitter straight off the tree, and must be pickled before they can be eaten. Many canned olives are dyed black with iron gluconate, which drastically reduces the nutritional value of the olives.

• Olive pits, mash, or pumace have been burned as fuel for thousands of years. Burned olives pits have been found in Jericho dating back over 5,000 years.

• A famous olive tree on the Mediterranean island of Crete, the "Olive of Vouves", is estimated to be from 2000 to 4000 years old.

• Olive trees are uniquely dependent upon humans for pruning. They cannot thrive without it. The entire top of an olive tree including branches and trunk can burn or be cut, but unless

the ground becomes hot enough to kill the roots, the tree will regenerate. An olive tree that is well-pruned can continue to regenerate from its roots virtually indefinitely, with a lifespan of two thousand years or longer.

• Wild olive trees can grow much larger and bushier than a pruned olive tree.

• Olive wood is excellent for carving small objects such as cups and spoons. The wood is generally not large enough for making furniture or building houses.

• The olive oil that miraculously burned for eight days when the Maccabees liberated Jerusalem from Greek rule in 165 BCE is still celebrated each year during the Jewish festival of light known as Chanukah, when foods rich in olive oil, such as latkes, are eaten.

• The emblem of the State of Israel shows a menorah with an olive branch on either side.

• Ein Zeitim (Hebrew for "Source of Olives" or "Spring of Olives") was a mixed Arab-Jewish village in the northern Galilee during the Middle Ages. In 1891, a group of Jewish settlers from Minsk, Belarus established a kibbutz there and planted olive groves and fruit orchards. In 1948, the Palmach were very active in the area as the city of Tzfat (Safed) became strategically crucial in the War of Independence.

• Olive oil contains important nutrients such as vitamin E, phenolic compounds, and essential fatty acids. It is thought to help protect against certain types of cancer, diabetes, heart attack, obesity, Alzheimer's disease, and inflammation.

• Olive leaves are known for their powerful healing properties. Olive leaf and olive leaf extracts (OLE), are now marketed as anti-aging, immunostimular, and antibiotic agents. Many reference books claim olive leaf extract is effective against viral infections, parasites, fungi, and even super-infections that resist antibiotics.

To find out more about olives, olive trees, and how this book was made, visit the author's book blog at
http://dyaelbernhard.com/bookblog/life-of-an-olive

www.ingramcontent.com/pod-product-compliance
Lightning Source LLC
Chambersburg PA
CBHW041636040426
42448CB00023B/3494